Buda Castle

László Gerő

Buda Castle

*Photos by
Lajos Dobos*

Corvina Kiadó

Title of the original:
A Budai Várnegyed, Corvina Kiadó, Budapest, 1979

Translated from the Hungarian by
Anna Bedárd
Maps by Tamás Biczó
Design by Vera Köböl

© Text: László Gerő, 1979
ISBN 963 13 0449 3

Printed in Hungary, 1979
Athenaeum Printing House, Budapest

It is difficult to know where to begin the story of the legendary settlement of Buda, for its houses recall a varied historical past spanning many centuries. It is difficult enough to describe, let alone describe succinctly all that the name 'Buda' means to the Hungarians. Many aspects need to be considered in a summary of the settlement's history. These include the origin and naming of the settlement, its modes of defence, the various efforts at castle construction by the rulers living here, the royal household, the University, the artists' workshops, the history of the crafts, the houses within the Castle area, the life and activities of the inhabitants, as well as the social and cultural development of the settlement. In other words, everything that is usually thought of as being part of a city.

The Hungarian capital, Budapest, was created in 1873 by the unification of three towns: Buda, Óbuda and Pest. Here, though, we are only concerned with the section of Budapest on the right bank of the Danube, and even of that, only the settlement lying on the Castle Hill of Buda, the former royal palace rising on its southern slope.

Like most Hungarian cities with a great historical past, the origin of Buda is also much debated. The founding of the city on Castle Hill—then called the New Hill of Pest—is often associated with the endeavours of Béla IV to construct fortresses for the country's defense after the Mongolian invasion (1241–1242). The queen's town, which lies at the foot of the hills across from the Island, was originally called Buda. Later, at the time of the initial castle construction, the new settlement on Castle Hill was called thus, while the older locality became known by the name of Óbuda (Old Buda).

Within the walls of the castle area is the Church of Our Lady, which is popularly known as the Matthias Church. On the basis of settlement patterns around the church in the Middle Ages, some infer that an earlier settlement core already existed at the time the church was constructed. The archaeological excavations of the entire area of Buda Castle, conducted after 1946, show that there was life on the plateau as early as a thousand years before the Romans. This is evidenced by the pits that are carved in rock within the Palace courtyard lying a few spans beneath the present roadbed near the Lion Gate.

It was not long before the Buda settlement became important throughout the country, and the geographical factors obviously played a decisive role. At this location, the Danube and the ancient trade route connecting East and West intersected. It was only here, by the New Hill (Castle Hill) along Devil's

Moat that it was possible to reach and cross the Danube. There were no suitable roads to the south because of marshes along the Danube, and to the north, because of the wooded hills of the Pilis Range.

Even the Romans realized the geographical significance of this locality. It is known that Marcus Aurelius, the famous emperor-philosopher, designated this spot as the seat of the imperial province of Pannonia. This took place at the time he conceived the boundary of the empire to be the Carpathians, which border the basin formed by the Danube and the Tisza. Later, the boundaries of the empire were the *limes* along the Danube, which were reinforced as a defence line.

After the Mongolian invasion, Béla IV (1235–1270) increased his efforts to centralize and strengthen the royal power. However, the threatening possibility of the Mongols' return forced him—at the expense of his power—to allow his lords to build castles. But, since Béla IV wanted to rely on the cities in his struggles against the oligarchy, he erected a castle on Buda Hill to support the adjoining settlement.

Those Hungarians and other inhabitants with various mother tongues who had survived the destruction of Pest, along with other foreigners from all parts of the world—Italian, French, Flemish, and many German settlers, comprised the new settlement. These people, together with their armed servants provided the defence of the city walls which were built at that time. Besides providing armed service, the city's entrepreneurs engaged in agriculture, especially viticulture, and commerce. This class was alien to Hungarian society at the time, but in Vienna the dominant strata of society, even in the middle of the 14th century, consisted of the descendants of these settlers. The royal castle complex was completed by 1255 and the city, now fortified with walls, was given a distinguished role.

The castle settlement founded by Béla IV began a quick course of development. This can be shown by the number of churches which were constructed at that time. The Church of Our Lady, the Church of Mary Magdalene, and the church of the Dominican monks, named after St. Nicholas, were all built between 1250 and 1260.

In the charter of 1244 given to the people of Pest, Béla IV re-established the legal rights and privileges of the people who settled in Pest and Buda. This determined the city's legal status, and at the same time, signified the close of an earlier phase of development. From this time on, it was not the Benedictines but **6** the mendicant friars of the Dominican and Franciscan orders who directed the construction workshops of Buda. Their works were influencial throughout all of Hungary. Everywhere the simplicity of the Dominican and Franciscan monks prevailed. The solid mass and slight articulation of the building's façade was characteristic of their style. There were buttresses, but not flying buttresses. The windows were also simple, with unarticulated openings. In these buildings the monumental portals and the many pillars and statues of the French Gothic were absent. Figural and ornamental decoration was found only on the pediment. No transepts, crossings, or towers over the crossings were built, and the nave was not divided into stories. The structure was simple, and the monastic chancel which extended lengthwise was developed early. From this unified concept of interior space evolved the hall churches. These churches were, in turn, the archetypes for the Renaissance architectural concept of space.

Béla IV fostered, to a great extent, the spread of the Dominican order and later the Franciscan order. On Margaret Island, he had a convent built in which his favourite daughter, Margaret, lived as a nun, and the Franciscan monastery of St. John the Evangelist within the castle walls. The Dominican church and monastery were also among the first constructions in Buda. These orders, of course, did everything possible to help Béla IV to carry through his great town-building program.

The construction workshop of Buda which developed in the 13th century may have been under the direction of the two mendicant orders. It soon became one of the outstanding centers for Central European Gothic architecture. The Church of Our Lady, later called either Matthias or Coronation Church, was built by this workshop between 1255 and 1269. At first, it was built with a 13-angle sanctuary which was closed in on seven sides. This architectural solution was characteristic of the early churches of the Dominican order. A similar arrangement for the chancel is found along the Rhine in France. The Dominican church that was begun in 1254 at Strasbourg and the Minorite church completed in 1260 at Cologne were built according to similar ground plans.

The Church of Our Lady of Buda was built in the French style with a polygonal chancel and side altars. The nave had four vault bays that were held up by three pairs of piers. The aisles were proportioned two to one, and there was a transept, which was not visible from the exterior, along with a southern portal and a vestibule flanked by a pair of towers on the west. Similar examples of this style can be found in Burgundy, Champagne, and on the Ile-de-France.

The ground plan, however, was already modified at the time of construction. The nave was built with only two pairs of piers in place of the planned three. The portal ornamentation resembled that of the Romanesque basilica of Ják in Transdanubia. The Mongol invasion (1241–1242) interrupted the building of the church. It is possible, that the workshop, which dispersed then, could have played a role in the formation of the *Riesentor* of the Viennese Stephanskirche. Other portions of the Church of the Blessed Virgin had characteristics of northern France (Reims, Amiens) through the mediating influence of Marburg and Trier. The purity of the naturalistic floral ornamentation in the church was the first such in the eastern half of Europe. French influence, observable in the works of the early Gothic workshop, is associated with master Villard de Honnecourt, whose sketch book documents his stay in Hungary around the time of the Mongol invasion. The large-scale reconstruction of the church in Buda probably began during the second half of the 14th century and lasted throughout the 15th century. At this time the splendid south portal, the Portal of Mary, was built with an open vestibule. Under King Matthias it was enlarged to include a royal oratory (1456–1460). Also at this time, the church's only tower was built with the Hunyadi family's coat of arms placed upon it. During the Turkish occupation its interior furnishings were destroyed, but in the Baroque period the church was remodelled several times.

The church received its current exterior, the new, magnificent stone-laced spire and the colourful glazed-tile roofing, almost one hundred years ago. At the same time, the chapels were remodelled, the interior redecorated and the new interior painted in the manner of the slightly pretentious restorations that were customary throughout Europe at the end of the last century. This work was conducted by a brilliant architect, Frigyes Schulek, in the years 1873–1896. Schulek gave the Gothic interior, slightly dismal to begin with, its strikingly colourful aspect which approximated the original colour effect.

The construction of the Dominican Church of St. Nicholas on what is today Hess András Square, preceded that of the Church of Our Lady. The monastic church was built around 1250, and its first abbot, Pál Pater, was a Hungarian who came from Bologna. The order also set up the *studium generale*, a school for advanced learning. The magnificent tombstones found on the floor of the sanctuary demonstrate how highly developed their stone sculpture workshop was at the time. Today, these can be seen in the barrel-vaulted basement room below the large Gothic hall in the Budapest Historical Museum. Among these   8 remains is the tombstone of the painter Abel, on which there is a Middle High German inscription from the year 1350, along with the artist's coat of arms with three empty escutcheons. The tomb of the French humanist Henry, decorated with a diagonally slanting lily, was also here. Also made during this same year were the tombs of Thomas, son of Michael, and Henry Pauher and others. In addition to the stone sculpture workshop, there was also a school for illuminators, whose outstanding artist, Péter Váci, illustrated St. Thomas Aquinas' work *Summa Theologiae* (Cathedral Library, Esztergom). The Dominican school in Buda Castle dealt with all the artistic pursuits. It was an interesting and distinctively medieval mixture of artistic endeavours, monastic traditions, and the system of guilds and workshops. The remains of the Church of St. Nicholas and the monastery, including the tower, the north wall of the nave, the cloister and the fountain, are today organic parts of the Hilton Hotel.

The Church of Mary Magdalene, built around 1274, is another renowned medieval building of Buda Castle. Located today on Kapisztrán Square—once known as the Saturday Market—the building was the Hungarian parish church before the Turkish invasion. During the Turkish occupation, the Christians were able to use only this one church, and even then only intermittently. The remains of its portal, in addition to the single-nave layout, indicate a hall church. Around the 1400s the church was enlarged into a three-aisle basilica. The sanctuary extended lengthwise and there was a single tower above its entrance as well as a chapel on either side. When the city was recaptured from the Turks in the year 1686, the church, which had been heavily damaged by cannon fire, was rebuilt in the Baroque manner. Unfortunately, it was again heavily damaged in 1944–1945. At this time the ruins of the nave were pulled down, leaving only the medieval tower with its beautiful lierne vault on the ground floor. In front of the entrance stands the small, Late Baroque vestibule designed by József Tallherr (1792). At the present time, the medieval remains of the church can be seen among the ruins.

Although little is known concerning the building activities of the Árpád dynasty, it is believed that the fortifications set up to guard the commercial trade route were the first constructions of a medieval royal palace. These fortifications were built on the southern tip of Castle Hill, and the *István* (Stephen) Castle and royal palace were built north of it. The remains of the medieval palace complex were only discovered and excavated within the last few decades.

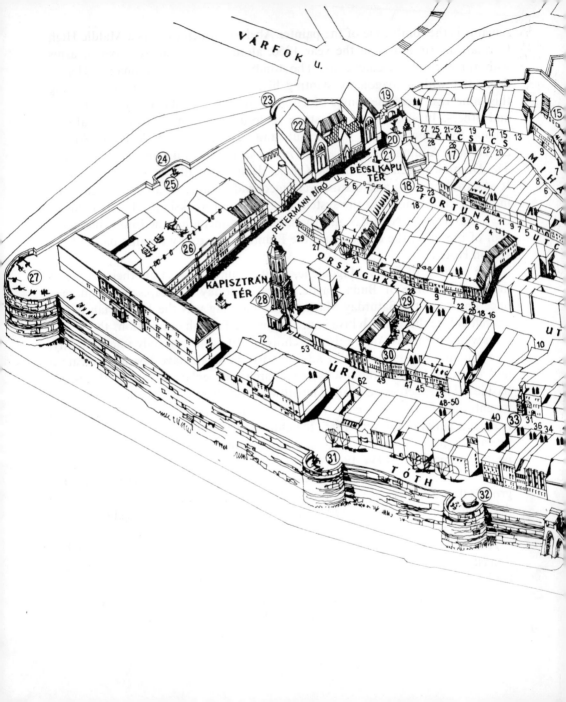

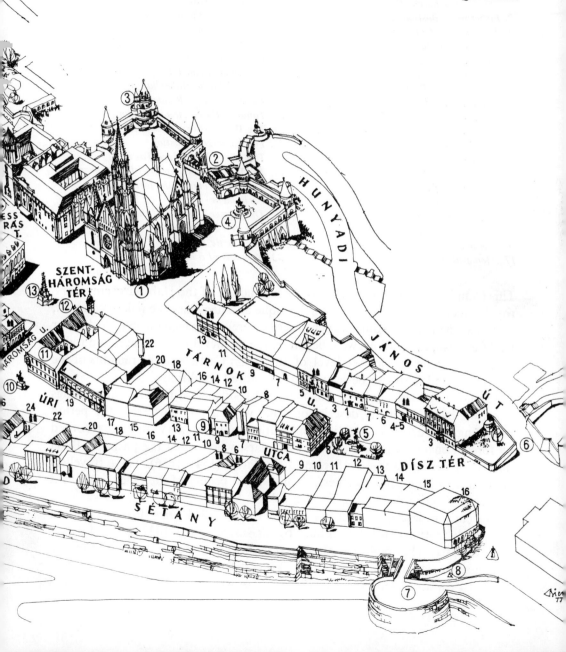

THE CASTLE HILL OF BUDA—VIEW OF THE CITIZENS' QUARTER

This complex had been buried by the construction of the Habsburg emperors' royal palace in Buda. However, the Baroque and neo-Baroque palace complex, as well as their surrounding gardens, were severely damaged during World War II. After 1946, excavations were begun on the medieval royal palace, and today a few rooms on the lowest level of the *István* Castle and the remains of the tower's ground floor can be seen in their restored condition.

The fame and splendour of this medieval residence of the Hungarian kings is known by some eighty descriptions that were left in part from the period preceding the Turkish occupation. In addition to these texts were those recorded by foreign envoys, or their chancery scholars, who visited the pasha of Buda during the century-and-a-half reign of the Turks (1541–1686). These travellers continued to praise the greatness, richness, and beauty of the place, even as it gradually deteriorated under Turkish rule.

The earliest descriptions highly praised the so-called *Friss* (Fresh) Palace, a large-scale Gothic construction built by Sigismund (1387–1437) of the Luxemburg dynasty. This building, already standing in 1419, surpassed the earlier buildings in size and ornamentation. Viewed from the town, the palace was fronted by a large courtyard; to the north of the palace, where the Matthias **12**

Fountain is located today, there lay a wide moat. The castle gate, reached by a stone bridge crossing the moat, was located on the western end of the castle wall. At that time, the arcaded formal courtyard was built between the *Friss* Palace and the old Little Courtyard. Its carved stones, made around the 1380s, show a relationship to the works of Prague's Parler workshop.

By this time, beyond the Little Courtyard to the south, the palace had been greatly enriched. The construction encompassed the earlier *István* Tower which had stood alone on the southern tip of the hill. King Sigismund, who was also the Holy Roman Emperor after 1410, wished to make Buda his befitting royal residence; this is why his palace was built on such a truly grand scale. Even by this time, the palace complex, which was expanded by the Gothic buildings of Sigismund, occupied a predominant place in the cityscape, which was to be characteristic of the area from this time on.

Two decades after the death of Sigismund, the diet of Pest, with the help of the lesser nobility, family friends, and the burghers of the town, elected Matthias (1458–1490) to be King of Hungary. Matthias was the son of János Hunyadi, the famous military leader who fought against the Turks. The centralized power of the king resting upon a strong mercenary army and a vast private estate, created one of Europe's richest courts. The annual revenue of Matthias was as much as a million ducats, surpassing at that time the revenue of either the English or the French king. From this time on, Buda was in fact the capital of the country.

Many artists and humanists from Italy enriched the luxurious life of the palace. The most famous of these was Bonfini, the historian of Matthias. Through men like these and through the young Hungarian nobles educated in Italy, the influence of the finest Renaissance architecture—that of Florence—spread to Hungary. In the workshops excellent illuminators, such as Cattaneo and Roselli, illustrated the famous 'Corvina' codices (in Latin *corvus* is the word for raven, the bird on Matthias' coat of arms). Works on the history of architecture by Alberti and Filarete (Antonio Averulino) can be found among these books. A work of Filarete displays a sketch of the Buda University planned by Matthias. The printing press of András Hess was also in operation at this time, and in 1473 he published the *Chronicle of Buda* in Latin.

Under the reign of King Matthias, the palace entered another period of large-scale construction. The second half of the 15th century was characterized by Late Gothic and Early Renaissance architecture. In raptured descriptions,

Bonfini recorded the construction activities of Matthias. From his accounts we know that Matthias' game preserve stood here, as well as a labyrinth and a marble aula with fountains and many other beautiful details. Bonfini writes that in Matthias' library, Latin and Greek works "are abundantly stacked, and the execution of the books is also lavish . . . The heavens can be seen on the vaults of one of the rooms, and he erected palaces which rival the pomp of the Romans. Here there are spacious dining rooms, excellently furnished bedrooms, and the gilded ceilings of various ornamentation and their floors laid in mosaics distinguish one room from another". He writes about bathrooms with cold and hot running water, lavishly decorated stoves, and life-size bronze statues.

Candelabras lined a wide, red marble staircase which led to a magnificent door with a richly carved frame. One of the candelabras can be seen today in the *Hagia Sophia* in Istambul. The splendid bronze leaves of the door were decorated on both sides with the feats of Hercules. This motif also occurs on the Renaissance fountain at Matthias' famous Visegrád palace, where the child Hercules can be seen grappling with the seven-headed Hydra of Lerna. Above the gate of the palace in Buda was a Latin epigram by Bonfini. According to his description, Matthias "appropriated vast sums for the ceilings, on whose sunken panels the chariots of the planets dash across the heavens". The arches of the arcaded courtyard were supported by slender, tall columns, and 12 constellations could be seen on the panelled ceiling of the loggia. In the middle of the courtyard, in front of the chapel, there was a marble fountain with a bronze statue of Pallas Athene. In the building adjoining the chapel were the vaulted rooms of the library where the famous Corvina Codices were placed on masterfully carved shelves.

The results of the extensive excavations conducted between 1946 and 1966 and a depot of medieval statues which was discovered in the northwest corner of the Palace in 1974, demonstrate that the descriptions of Matthias' contemporaries cannot be considered simply as the customary flattering of courtiers. The foreign envoys would have no reason to exaggerate their reports. It is therefore unfortunate that the remains of the royal court are so fragmentary. However, these fragments are enough to tell of the unusually high artistic standard of the lodges who worked on the royal constructions, the stone carving, ceramic and majolica workshops of the Buda Court. A fine example of this workmanship is a charming and beautiful head of a girl exhibited in the **14** corridor leading to the Chapel, which was carved around 1360 by János Master, the "royal stone sculptor". Even more precious than this is the rich series of statues brought to light in the course of the 1974 excavations. The secular figures can be seen in the restored Great Hall, and the ecclesiastical figures, in the Chapel.

These statues which must have been discarded sometime between 1430 and 1475, were found among the remains of a small house which had been filled in with the refuse of the royal court at the time of a large-scale construction. The location is marked by the remains of the "Beggars' Gate", currently displayed on St. George Square. After the initial find, an additional 50–55 medieval torsos were discovered. They were made of soft Hungarian limestone and were of various sizes. Originally, they might have formed a unified group. Most of the figures are well made, and are strikingly portrait-like, the work of court sculptors who were the best of their age. The ecclesiastical figures are generally smaller than the secular ones. They may have decorated a modest-size chapel. These statues were probably executed by travelling artisans around 1450. They differed from the works of the Viennese and Prague schools, for they were manifestations of the Early Renaissance, a new artistic trend spreading from Italy through Avignon to Burgundy.

The stone cutters of the royal construction workshop were also excellent workmen. The beautiful architectural layout of the Gothic Great Hall and the beautifully carved window frames in the Castle Museum are only two examples of their work. The magnificent carvings from hard red limestone which are exhibited in the Renaissance Hall should also be mentioned. Among these is a fine Florentine Renaissance capital and a white hard limestone door casing which shows Matthias' raven with a ring in his beak. This work recalls one of the great masters of the Italian Renaissance, Francesco di Giorgio Martini, who was also a famous castle architect. He built the palace at Urbino for Federigo da Montefeltre, who was a great patron of Renaissance humanism. The Renaissance door frame in the Buda palace shows a remarkable resemblance to those made by the Da Maiano brothers for the Urbino Palace. The carvings ordered by Matthias are excellent works done in the Florentine tradition. No other examples resembling this style have been found outside of Italy.

The palace's water supply system was probably constructed by Aristotele Fioravanti of Bologna. The system of hydraulics which carried the water from **15** the Danube to the top of Castle Hill was probably his work as well.

Also present in the Renaissance Hall of the present Budapest Historical Museum are the original coloured glazed floor tiles. Only at the Vatican, in the former apartments of Pope Alexander Borgia VI who was of Spanish origin, are there floor tiles which can be compared with those in Buda. The hexagonal tiles in Buda are similar in shape to those made on the Spanish coast around 1450. However, only blue designs on a white base are found on the tiles from Spain (Al Murci), while in Buda, green, yellow and blue are used to decorate the tiles. The tiles also incorporate the symbols of the Aragon dynasty, from which Beatrice, Matthias' second wife, descended. The Aragonese coat of arms is found on the exquisite escutcheon of the Renaissance Hall, and also alongside Matthias' coat of arms on the garden fountain.

The coloured glazed tile roofing and the gilded, sphere-like ceramic ornamentation placed on the spires enhanced the magnificent appearance of the palace complex. Upon arriving in Buda, the famous 17th-century Turkish traveller, Evliya Chelebi, gave thanks to Allah for having been able to see the "*Kizil elma* (Golden Apple) Palace". The Turkish name for the palace refers to the ornamentation on the roof.

In the barrel-vaulted rooms of the *István* Castle, a small number of artifacts provide a glimpse of the life of the royal court in medieval Hungary. There are numerous pieces which resemble Dutch stove tiles, several of which depict a dragon-like monster encircling family crests. These undoubtedly refer to Sigismund's "Order of the Dragon", a league of nobles who allied themselves to the king and who helped to strengthen his power. On one of the brown glazed tiles, Sigismund is depicted with his forked beard. Another more colourful tile, depicts Matthias on his throne.

There are other remains from the medieval royal palace. Besides the *István* Tower and a few barrel-vaulted rooms of *István* Castle, the Great Hall still remains from the original palace. The interior portion was protected by a wall four meters wide that was built after 1686 to ward off Turkish attack.

The ground floor of the Great Hall is an 11-metre-wide, barrel-vaulted room of considerable size. It houses the exhibition of Gothic tombstones from the Dominican Church of St. Nicholas. Piers constructed from beautifully carved stones support the six groin vaults of the ceiling. These Gothic ribs and keystones of the vaults were buried in the basement. Luckily, they were uncovered, and together with the imposts and arches from the piers, they were reinstated in their original position.

16

Another feature of the Great Hall is its richly carved cross windows, which resemble those decorating the Palazzo Venezia in Rome. Fortunately, parts of one, together with an attached sedile, have remained in their original positions. Along with these it was also possible to reinstate the lower level of the two-story palace chapel. This chapel, named after St. John the Almsgiver, includes a small choir with three tracery windows. The windows resemble those in the City Parish Church of Pest, which was converted into a hall church during the reign of Sigismund.

If the restored Gothic Hall—which was by no means the largest in the medieval palace complex of Buda—and the ground floor of the chapel, along with a few lower rooms of the *István* Castle, do not even approximate the original design, they at least give the visitor a basis on which to imagine the one-time massive, towering Gothic royal palace with its coloured enamel tile roofing. At the very least, it is hoped that the atmosphere of the palace has been recreated; the palace praised by Bonfini, the humanist historian of King Matthias, and many others—Enea Silvio Piccolomini, later Pope Pius II—among them.

At the same time, the stern, unfriendly atmosphere of the deep gardens among the palace remains and the surrounding castle walls were eased by reconstructing the one-time decorative gardens of the castle courtyards which were once divided into three sections by the walls. The aim was to recreate the way these gardens must have looked at the time of Sigismund and Matthias, to have them emanate the same historical atmosphere which has been preserved in the medieval ruined walls.

These reconstructions, however, should not be confused with the later and better known Renaissance and Baroque gardens. Even Italy's best known and most ancient gardens (the *Giardino Boboli* in Florence, the *Villa d'Este* in Tivoli, and the garden of the *Villa Aldobrandini* in Frascati) date only from the Baroque period, with perhaps certain Renaissance traditions intact. Those from the Middle Ages did not survive even in Italy except for a few cloisters or *chiostro*.

We know about the vegetation of medieval gardens in Hungary from old documents and about the form of such gardens from the Flemish paintings of masters like the Van Eyck brothers, Rogier van der Weyden, Memling and Dirk Bouts. Though they usually depicted interiors, their windows often opened unto portions of medieval gardens. Flower beds located on high walls, tall, narrow flower planters at the base of the walls, and rose arbors are found in these gardens. In every instance, the flower beds are always arranged in geometric forms.

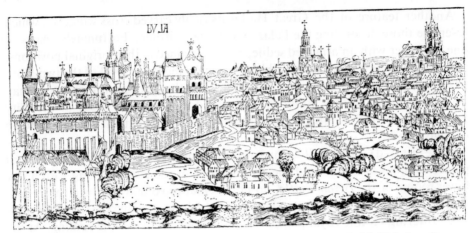

1. *Buda Castle. Woodcut by Michael Wolgemut, from Hartmann-Schedel*, Weltchronik, Nuremberg, 1493

The square monastery courtyard with a fountain in the middle is also of medieval origin. The plants, lilies, lilies-of-the-valley, thyme, roses, pomegranate, figs, sorb trees, almonds and hazelnuts, all ease the grim effect of the stone walls.

After restoration, the medieval castle walls surrounding the royal palace approximate the Buda of the Master Wolgemut, as can be seen on a woodcut (made after a drawing from 1470) in the *World Chronicle* Hartmann-Schedel printed in Nuremberg. The woodcut was not considered historically accurate for a long period of time because it depicted frame houses in Víziváros (Water Town) in Buda, and such houses were never built in Hungary. Today, however, its principal details, which include the palace complex, are accepted as authentic. It is possible to recognize, for example, the transverse situation of the *István* tower. In addition, the master correctly depicts the palace chapel, one of the square towers with its Gothic bay-window, as well as the similar bay-window of the Great Hall. In the course of the excavations, the stone pediment that had toppled down on the ground in front of the palace was also brought to light, the row of stones forming the crown were once held together by an iron which anchored the pediment to the building.

The round South Bastion or Rondella, an early example of the spread of firearms and fortification with cannons for castle defense, was possibly built **18**

List of Plates

during the reign of King Matthias to protect the medieval royal palace complex. It is believed that Italian engineers built the bastion, as in the case of the similar round Bocar Bastion at Ragusa (Dubrovnik). This structure was built by Michelozzo Michelozzi in the 1450s. The former name of the round South Bastion, *Baluardo d'Italia*, also tends to support this theory.

The ground plan of the medieval palace, including the most recently restored Gothic Main Hall, can currently be explained. In the opinion of László Gerevich, director of the excavations, the *Friss* (Fresh) Palace did not face the Danube, but faced north. Walls and a moat separated it from the town and enclosed an open area. It is possible that this arrangement was similar to that of the hippodrome where chariot races and other games were held in front of the Byzantine imperial palace.

After this open area, which is called the Buda Grounds, and which lies in front of the castle gate, the houses of the town continued to the north. On the Danube side there was the Franciscan monastery, which was later the residence of the pasha of Buda. Also, here was the small provostal church of St. Sigismund and next to it was the Jewish street. Then came St. George Square and a small church of the same name. This area is currently known as the *Dísz* or Parade Square, and the statue of the National Guardsman now stands in place of the church. Its sanctuary faced east as did those of the other medieval churches of the Castle District.

The beautifully proportioned square leads into the dwelling quarter of the castle. These protracted streets run north and south and are roughly parallel to the western Long Wall. While these long streets and short intersecting alleyways are not completely symmetrical, they are still not as twisted as those characteristic of a non-planned medieval town. Upon examination of the division of the plots facing the street, it becomes evident just how symmetric they really are. The frontal width of the majority of these plots can be traced back to a single measurement of approximately 18 metres. Only in a few cases were these plots divided into half, or later on in the Baroque period, merged. These characteristics suggest a planned city. For this reason, it is believed that the settlement of Buda Castle was built as a homogeneous project by the new settlers (1250). This method of building was customary elsewhere at that time, for example, in Vienna.

The Castle District has preserved the medieval anatomy of its streets; thus the relatively small houses and wide streets generate a characteristic that can be called distinctly Hungarian. This is possible because in Prague, Vienna, and the other medieval towns of Italy and other western European countries, the streets are not nearly as wide and the walls are much taller. In Buda, among the elongated and relatively wide streets, an unusually wide one can be found. This is Tárnok Street, which begins at the former St. George (Parade) Square which, similarly to *Breite Strasse* of Magdeburg, may have served as a market place in the Middle Ages.

Though there are elements in Castle District which seem to be distinctly Hungarian, the houses have their counterparts in other cities. These houses, with their wide façades and central doors, are similar to those owned by travelling tradesmen-merchants in Prague.

Research launched after the 1944–1945 war damages found that the bulk of the houses in the Buda Castle settlement originate from the time of Sigismund. Among these houses are Nos. 9, 18, 20 on Országház Street and Nos. 29–31, 32, 33, 61–66 on Úri Street. The remains of interior and exterior wall paintings prove that the houses were decorated with brightly coloured, black, white and green designs. This would have given the entire cityscape a gay appearance. An example of this manner of decoration is the façade of No.14, Tárnok Street. This façade was restored from hundreds of original palm-sized fragments to reproduce the pleasant medieval effect.

The 1412 description of the house in Buda of the family of nobles called Garai will perhaps shed light on life-style in the Middle Ages. This house had a dining room, living room and pantry on the first floor, and a painted dining room, chapel and pantry on the second. While this home no longer exists, at 31, Úri Street there is a three-storied Gothic house which still stands. At 18, 20, 22, Országház Street and 14, Tárnok Street, there are still two-storied Gothic Houses.

The Turks did very little building in the Buda Castle District, even though the head of the conquered territory, the pasha of Buda, resided here. Interestingly enough, he did not choose to reside in the royal palace, which remained vacant. Instead, he chose to live in the medieval Franciscan monastery near today's Castle Theatre. The *janissaries*, the Sultan's guard, located themselves around the pasha. The majority of the dwellings were occupied by the Turkish garrison. Since the soldiers were often replaced, little attention was given to the maintenance of the houses, which eventually became uninhabitable. Instead, the Turks fortified the surrounding castle walls even more, and within them they set up **20**

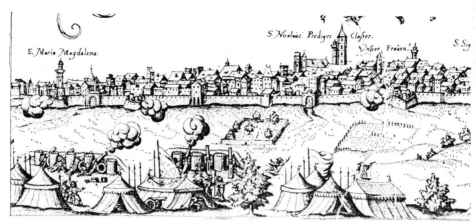

2. Detail of an etching by J. Siebmacher, c. 1600

3. View of Buda and Pest from the west. Detail of an engraving by Matheus Merian, Sr., 1638

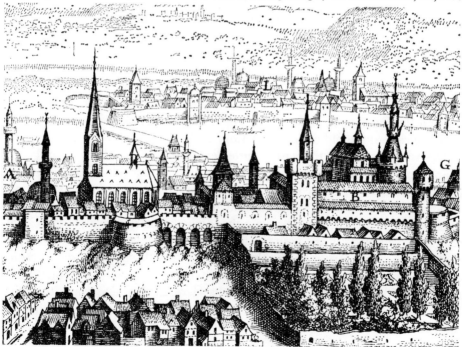

wooden booths. From the Constantinople travel journal of H. Dernschwamm (1553), it is known that those booths filled the middle of the wide street mentioned above.

The round *Fehérvári* Bastion, the "Bastion of Pasha Kasim", can be traced back to the Turkish defense constructions. The massive structure, 50 metres in diameter, was built to defend the *Fehérvári* Gate. According to an engraved inscription on a memorial tablet, Pasha Gürdji Kenan began construction on the bastion in 1650. (When Chelebi saw the bastion, it was only two metres high.) It was finished under the direction of Pasha Kasim in 1666–1667. The Tower of Pasha Karakas, which was built between 1618 and 1621, is also of Turkish origin. The castle wall facing the Buda Hills, the Long Wall, is fortified with round bastions that were presumably built according to the plans of the Turkish engineer Siavus Aga.

In 1686, after four unsuccessful attempts, the united Christian armies recaptured Buda from the Turks. But they succeeded only after a 75-day siege, and at the price of the town's appalling destruction.

In the city recaptured from the Turks, the united armies celebrated the success of the long, hard siege with bonfires, and the little that had remained was burned to the ground. Over several decades, the town slowly returned to life, preserving the Middle Ages in its layout and structure, but mainly in the remains of the walls of the ground floors. However, the façade of the renewed city was Baroque. Even now, many remains of the older architectural periods are hidden under a Baroque guise. Thus, remains have been preserved much the same way as in the case of the old buildings in Rome.

The wide streets of the castle settlement have already been described as characteristically Hungarian. However, the Gothic period of **Buda** has still another feature that may be considered characteristic of **Hungary**, i.e. the various kinds of *sedilia* that are found in a number of doorways. Scholars disagree about their origin. There are those who relate the origin of the Gothic sedilia in the houses of the bourgeoisie to the wine trade, which was important in medieval towns. According to the archives of Bártfa, Sopron, and Pozsony, the wine trade was extremely important in Hungarian towns, amounting to more than 50% of the total value of trade. Here, in their doorways, the privileged burghers dispensed their wine. But, the *sedilia* are not found exclusively in the houses of burghers, and there are many varieties. In Buda, more than 40 doorways with these *sedilia* are known. Still, if they are related to the wine 22

4. Buda in 1686. Engraving by M. Wening after a drawing by L. N. W. Hallart. Detail

trade, the question poses itself: Why are they not found in either Vienna or Prague? Wine trade existed there as well.

The use of the *sedilia* in Buda is much more likely to be traced back to local custom. Among the dwellings of medieval Buda there were many keeps in the Middle Ages. One such keep has recently been uncovered at 37–39, Úri Street,

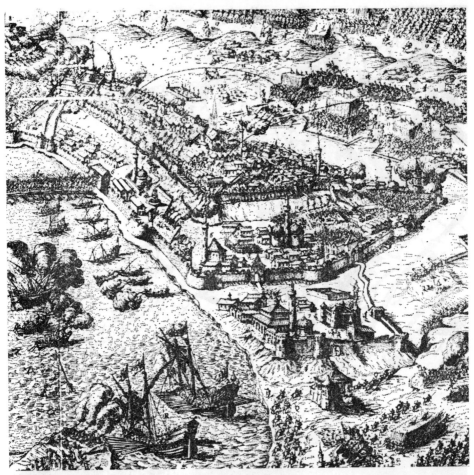

5. *Detail of an engraving by Gian-Giacomo de Rossi, 1687*

and in a 17th-century print by Siebmacher, six or seven similar keeps are visible north of the Church of Our Lady. During the period of feudal anarchy, some families may have isolated themselves in these towers as a result of family feuds. (Entire groups of these towers characterized 13th-century Italian towns, for example, Florence and Bologna, some of which have remained, such as those in San Gimignano.) On the ground floor of these defense towers, *sedilia* 24 for the guards are often found. In Buda, remains from such towers may have been incorporated into dwellings later on. In this way the use of *sedilia* could have spread and become an architectural feature of Buda in the Gothic period. Certainly, nowhere else are these stone benches used to such a great extent. This fashion may have influenced the architecture of other Hungarian towns such as Sopron, as well.

In most cases, these beautifully formed *sedilia* came to light not long ago, in the midst of the destruction caused by World War II, since in the 18th century, the Baroque guise built upon the medieval remains concealed everything that was old. Medieval details—*sedilia*, the carved stones of door and window frames—were revealed once again and became important as evidence from the Middle Ages. These remnants, scattered throughout the town, substantiate the origin of the entire settlement. For this reason, they are more important than the generally accepted architectural practice which refrains from preserving the traces of different periods on a single façade in pursuit of a unified style, hiding the medieval origins of the settlement. For example, the Gothic remains found on the third floor of 31, Úri Street make it apparent that not only low or single-storied dwellings stood in medieval Buda.

Impeded by frequent epidemics, fires, and floods, the rebuilding of Buda was to await the Baroque period. The engineer of the Treasury, Prati, reported in 1714 that there were only 151 houses rebuilt and 64 still in ruins. In the beginning, the architects were Italians—Ceresola, F. de Prati, A. E. Martinelli—and only later Austrians—J. Hölbling, A. Mayerhoffer, M. Nepauer, G. Paur, F. A. Hillebrandt, and others. Between 1710 and 1718, a water-supply system was built according to the plan of Kirschensteiner, a Jesuit father. This system brought the spring waters of the Buda Hills to the Castle settlement.

The significance of the Castle settlement will not be found in the artistic and historical worth of individual buildings. Still, there are certain remnants among them that are especially interesting. These include the barrel vaults of *Balta köz* (Balta alleyway), the doorway of the *Vörös Sün* (Red Porcupine) house in Hess András Square, the numerous Gothic *sedilia*, the massive Gothic arcades of the courtyard at 2, Országház Street, and the remains of medieval synagogues in Táncsics Street. Especially valuable are the tasteful details of the Baroque and Late Baroque palaces and dwellings. For example, 5, Országház Street is known not only for its façade, but also for its doorway, staircase, and courtyard.

25 Today the streetscapes in the Castle District of Buda are predominantly

Baroque, but they do not remind one of the Austrian imperial city, Vienna, nor of Prague, both known for their richly articulated palace façades. The Buda buildings differ considerably as they are simple variations of a very modest bourgeois Baroque.

While most of the buildings are fairly simple, there are a few outstanding Baroque palaces of significant size, such as *Batthyány* palace at 3, Dísz Square, or *Erdődy* palace at 7, Táncsics Mihály Street. Built between 1692 and 1774 according to the plans of architects Venerio Ceresola and Máté Nepauer, the Old Town Hall of Buda at 2, Szentháromság Street is of outstanding artistic quality. The same high quality is found in the former House of Parliament (28, Országház Street), which was designed by Franz Anton Hillebrandt and built in 1784. Its exquisite façade resembles the buildings surrounding the Viennese *Josephsplatz*.

Hillebrandt also designed the new royal palace, which predominates the Buda townscape. The ruins of the medieval palace were carried away, and the courtyard between the building and the castle walls were filled in seven–eight metres deep with rubble covering up the medieval portions that were brought to the surface only after 1946. In place of the luxurious medieval palace, a modest Baroque castle, resembling barracks rather than a royal residence, was erected at the beginning of the 18th century. The king never lived in it, only the Austrian commanding officer for military administration. In the second half of the century, during the reign of Maria Theresa (1740–1780), this insignificant building was enlarged into a palace. By the end of the century, a middle projection of the façade decorated with rows of columns in Late Baroque looked out on the Danube. To the north of this, at the site of the present Museum of the Working Class Movement, stood an arsenal, the Baroque *Zeughaus*, with its main façade facing St. George Square.

However, the emperor, residing in Vienna, did not need this lovely Baroque palace, so it became the temporary home for the university which was moving at the time from Nagyszombat. At a later date the palatine, who was the Hungarian high commissioner and resident for the Austrian emperor, lived here.

During the 1848–1849 War of Independence, Hungarian soldiers besieged the castle which was occupied by the Austrian military. During the siege the palace was burned down, but it was soon restored. After the Compromise of 1867 between the Hungarian Diet and the Austrian Imperial House, the Austrian emperor was also crowned king of Hungary, and the palace of Maria

6. Architectural history of the baroque palace after 1686

1 Building from the time of Charles III, 1715–1738
2 Palace from the time of Maria Theresa, 1749–1770, Hölbling–De Prati
2/a Weapons arsenal (Zeughaus)
3 Expansion planned by Ybl, 1881–1891
4 Expansion planned by Hauszmann, 1891–1902

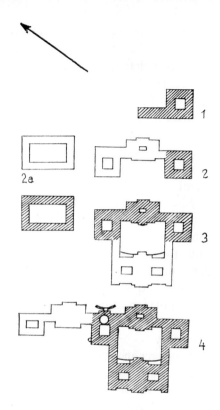

Theresa proved to be too small for the ceremonies. For this reason, and also because the imperial court resided here several times after 1867, Francis Joseph I (1848–1916) decided to enlarge it.

In 1881, Miklós Ybl, who had designed the Opera House, was commissioned to enlarge the palace. He designed a new building adjoining the palace of Maria Theresa and facing *Krisztinaváros* (Christina Town). It consisted of two small wings attached to the old palace. On one of these wings facing the town, the so-called Lion Gate, with sculptures by János Fadrusz was constructed. The Ybl addition, together with the old palace, created a beautiful, large, walled-in courtyard. However, it covered so much ground that it could not be accommodated on Castle Hill's southern plateau. Because the plateau narrows at this end, Ybl was forced to extend the wing westward so that it face the Buda Hills. He severed the medieval castle wall which had surrounded Castle Hill in order to lay the new building's foundation. The foundation was to contain a number of basement levels, but Ybl died in 1891 and only saw the ground story completed. His successor, Alajos Hauszmann, continued to enlarge the palace. He doubled the size of the Danube façade, and to emphasize the corner in front of the Lion Gate, he designed a beautiful fountain with sculptures by Alajos Stróbl, one of which is the figure of King Matthias.

Hauszmann kept the rhythmic pattern of the windows and the sills of the Baroque building, but his art nouveau, Late-Eclectic arrangement of details, especially on the new cupola, was not successful. To understand the new Hauszmann façade, it is necessary to know that, instead of the single, protruding middle projection of the Maria Theresa palace, two separate projections were built. The new medial axis fell between the projections. It was necessary to counterbalance the exceedingly lengthened horizontal block of the new façade, while the uncertain medial axis needed emphasis. Hauszmann wanted to resolve these problems by placing a new cupola on the medial axis. For the same reason, he employed a playful resolution for the roofs, using many little mansard corner cupolas, and emphasized the attic window architecture. Reshaped in this fashion, the palace complex has since become a characteristic element of Buda's cityscape.

Before reconstruction of the palace complex began, a plan was proposed to maintain the ruins as a permanent reminder of the senseless destruction of war. However, the volume of the building's ruins, 70,000 cubic metres, would have been too large, not to mention its central locality in the townscape, nor the unattractive spectacle of the ruins. Finally, it was decided to completely restore the complex; furthermore, reconstruction offered a chance to carry out research which reconfirmed the historical importance of the buildings.

In the beginning there was also talk of simplifying to some extent the mass of the palace. The building complex, however, was soon revealed to be a well conceived aggregate, whose disruption would only have an adverse effect on its parts. For this reason, it was decided to retain the original foundations. After 1945, restoration work concentrated on re-establishing the more simple exterior of the original Baroque building, to re-establish the palace's effect on the townscape, and the Budapest Historical Museum, the National Gallery, and the Museum of Modern History were soon housed within the complex.

In addition to the Baroque-style palace, the bulk of the dwellings in Castle District also reflect the Baroque period. Besides the exterior façades of the **28** streets in the district, the courtyards of the houses offer a special attraction. These courtyards are lovely not so much because of their architectural design, but because of their atmosphere and charming little gardens.

Many moments of history are invoked by Buda. The castle walls which enclose the settlement, the tower of Pasha Karakas, the *Savanyú leves* (Sour Soup) Bastion, the *Fehérvári* and *Esztergomi* round bastions, the *Bécsi* (Viennese), *Vízi* (Water), and *Fehérvári* gates, recall the times preceding the 1686 recapture of the castle, the abortive sieges, and the memorable Turkish ploy which played Buda into Turkish hands in 1541. The former Water Tower recalls the system by which the castle was supplied with water, the Danube waterway which supported the inhabitants, and its defensive wall leading up from the tunnel along the Ellipse Walkway. But the castle wells and cisterns, the stables and coach houses which were plentiful at one time, also come to mind. The burghers, the various kinds of craftsmen and traders, along with peasants from near-by vineyards and ploughlands, all needed water. The creators of the first Baroque waterworks, for example, directed the spring waters from the surrounding hills into the castle area.

Castle District suffered great damage during 1944–1945. Since that time, only praise can be offered for those endeavours and projects aimed at systematically revealing the historical value of this part of the city. These endeavours were manifold. One of the aims was to demolish the exceedingly massive structures from the turn of the century which did not fit into the smaller aggregates of the castle dwellings. The damaged condition of the former ministerial buildings aided this endeavour. It was primarily because of their ruinous state that all the ministries were relocated around the Parliament building in the governmental district of Pest after the war. This made it possible to reduce the number of large-size buildings in the historic ensemble. Still, the restoration and urbanization of the castle area did not stop here. There were regulations about new buildings and the boundaries of the old lots, and there were strict laws to preserve the unity of extant neighbouring buildings and the profiles of adjoining roofs. At the end of World War II, though, when there was an enormous housing shortage, great care was taken with the areas of the Castle District which were in ruins. This only demonstrates the importance of the palace complex to Hungarian culture.

The first measures taken were to save the remains of the ruined buildings, **29** but another primary concern was the favourable transformation of the roofs

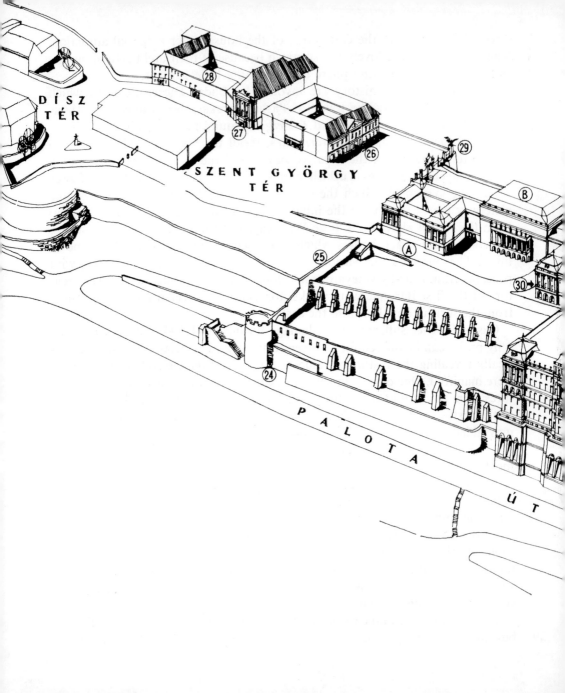

DÍSZ TÉR

SZENT GYÖRGY TÉR

PALOTA ÚT

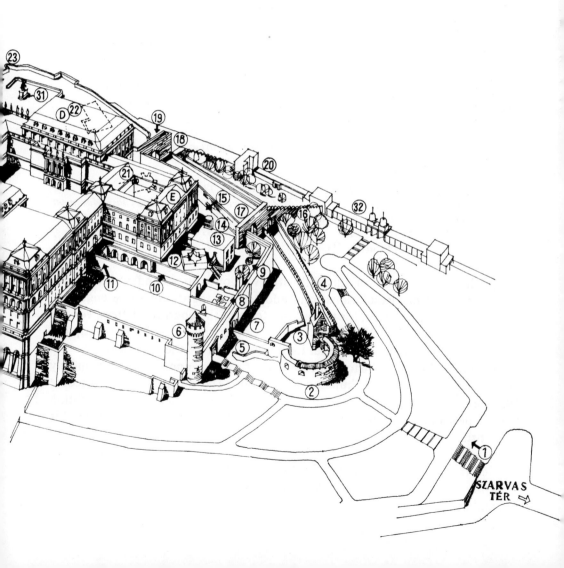

SZARVAS
TÉR

through the elimination of unsightly attic windows, doors and walkways for chimney sweeping. Resolutions were adopted for the use of stone engraving for house and street signs, for the antique form of the engraved letters, for the use of gas for public lighting, and for many other small details. These stipulations all contributed to the special local atmosphere of the historical city.

The protection of the historical ensemble of a city cannot be realized merely through the adoption of building restrictions. The present city has become what it is today as part of a continual process of development. The termination of this development would only condemn either all or part of the city and this is not the purpose of preserving monuments. The historical nucleus of the city must continue to meet the new demands of life. For example, families often moved from the crowded inner city to healthier, greener areas. As a result of this process, the most valuable sections of the inner city became its most neglected and depopulated parts.

Thus, in order to preserve the city's historical nucleus, those new demands of modern life must be found and met which will benefit the city today as well as in the future. Only in this way and not by the mummification or transformation of the city into a museum, is it possible to justify the preservation of monuments in the city.

The historical environment can be a "human island" in the dehumanizing atmosphere of the big city even if the individual buildings are not first-rate monuments. In fact, in Hungary, the typical historical core of a city is not made up of valuable buildings. Rather, it reveals its old, often medieval origin in the lines of its streets, its walls, and in the shape of its squares. Yet at the same time, this is where the greatest number of monuments are located in the area.

How did the preservation of Buda take place? In the course of the restoration of the historical city nucleus defined by the medieval castle walls, it was necessary to go from house to house and bring each individual building up to date. In places, the irretrievably obsolete portions and the more recent courtyard additions had to be either demolished or renovated. With the elimination of certain portions, the city quarter was able to obtain more fresh air and sunlight. In the midst of renewal, though, it was imperative to retain the historical character and unadulterated atmosphere of the area.

The Hungarian standpoint concerning new developments in the spaces where there were collapsed and unrestorable buildings, or buildings plundered by earlier reconstruction evolved with the help of several experiments in Castle District. Based on these, it was considered undesirable to build counterfeits in the historical environment. Even at the beginning of the Buda Castle restoration in 1950, the use of archaisms was excluded, so as not to detract from the value of the originals. But it also seemed inappropriate to erect neutral buildings in the old environment, as was done during the 1930s at the proposal of Professor G. Giovannoni around the *Piazza Argentina* in Rome. A total of 60 buildings were needed in the castle area, and if neutral houses were built in all these spaces in addition to those built in Buda between 1950 and 1956, they would soon constitute a separate grouping of their own. Thus, there was the danger that, forming such a considerable group, they would forcefully disrupt the townscape. According to the Hungarian viewpoint that had evolved by the end of the 1950s, it was decided that the façade of a new building built in the historical complex was to express the age of its construction, or in other words, it should be a modern building as was its predecessor in its own time. Nevertheless,

33

it was to conform unconditionally to its surroundings, primarily to the old lot divisions and to the mass, roof shape and roofing material of the neighbouring houses. If possible, they were also to conform in the articulation of their façades. Also, care was taken not to build one large unit on what were once several smaller plots which would overpower the extant smaller buildings. Such buildings, which do not conform to the old scale of the town, shatter the atmosphere of an old city most easily.

The character and atmosphere of Buda consists of many factors, and most of these are hard to define. These include the buildings, the old, medieval city walls, ditches, and gates or the spots where they once were, the network of streets and squares, the bends and curves of the streets, the old lot divisions, the height of the buildings, the horizontal rows of houses and the vertical emphasis of the towers, as well as the small alleyways and stairs. There are many surprises that can be found by a passer-by. The small, closed-in squares, restful benches, trees and other plants combine to produce a pleasing effect. The character of the city is found in the pavement, the lighting, the people who rush or stroll on the streets, the cordiality and cheerfulness of the inhabitants, the array and refinement of the shops and their display windows, the open doorways looking into courtyards—one of Buda's principal charms—the street vendors and their stands, and the playing children. The character and atmosphere of a city are also shaped by order and cleanliness, or by neglect; think of the meticulousness of Holland's dazzlingly clean streets, for example, or the picturesque disorder of the Mediterranean settlements.

Other factors in the Castle District's atmosphere are the many fragrances and aromas of the city, the vegetable and fruit markets, the flower stands, the city in sunlight or rain, or even covered by snow. Every detail can be important in this overall picture. This is why neon signs, advertisements, and posters were avoided.

In maintaining the historical building complex of Buda, the above mentioned factors were given primary consideration. The restoration of the monument buildings was the most important task, but first, research on the architectural history of the buildings had to be completed. Only plans which were based on authentic records won official approval. The preservation of the historically valuable buildings was an important task, but beyond this, the designer had to include proposals for their renovation. The obsolete, damp dwellings needed to be brought up to date, to become well-ventilated, sunlit apartments. In this way, the unique problems of restoring the monuments were combined with attempts to meet present-day requirements. This naturally included the renovation of public utilities, as well as solving the problem presented by the additional wings that had been built in the courtyards. If the wings were damaged, these were not allowed to be rebuilt; in this way, the courtyards received more fresh air and sunlight.

There were no conceptual difficulties in restoring the monuments; they were merely restored following the general practice that was in effect throughout the country. Only the new developments which would occupy the vacant lots offered an opportunity for discussion. The type of new architecture which should be placed into a historical environment was problematic throughout Europe and is still debated today. However, the first new buildings of Buda were erected in the early 1950s according to the principle of "neutrality". These buildings, acclaimed in the historical complexes of Italy, are reservedly neutral buildings which do not duplicate any historical style, that is, they neither archaicize, nor are they modern; they exist somewhere between the two.

After the first dozen neutral houses were built in Buda—among them 12, Úri Street, 4–5, Dísz Square, 10, Tárnok Street—it became painfully evident that in the Buda complex, where there were so many historical periods and styles, only modern architecture was not represented. Instead of allowing the introduction of modern buildings, the authorities responsible for the protection of the monuments insisted on the invented, architecturally worthless neutral houses, which sooner or later would have become dominant among the various older architectural styles.

After this was realized, the presence of modern architecture was no longer rejected in the architectural complex of the Castle district. The new form of architecture obviously has a "style" of its own. Naturally, certain limitations are still in effect today, such as the size of the buildings, the form of the roofs and the fashion of roofing, and the preservation of the existing row of houses.

Since 1956, numerous works of modern architecture can be found in conjunction with the historical houses. There are some extremely successful examples, such as the houses at 32, Úri Street and, most recently, 4 and 10, Úri Street, whose windows suggest the same vertical rhythmic pattern as those of the historical buildings. The houses at 16, Fortuna Street and 6, Országház Street are also fine examples. However, other houses incorporate horizontal emphasis in their windows. These are slightly detached from the overall rhythm of the Buda

Castle complex, for example 9, Dísz Square, and the school at 9–11, Tárnok Street. There is even a new house in the Castle complex (9–11, Szentháromság Street) which has the structure of a framed building as well as a frontal roster, but is only two storeys high. From the structural, architectural point of view, this is unjustified, and is a needless contradiction of the character of the older houses. It would have made more sense if the drainage from the high roof of the house had been resolved with the help of a ledge, rather than an attic. The same unresolved details which characterize the façade facing Úri Street are also found on the façade of the house at 8, Dísz Square, even though both houses are excellently planned and well thought out. Other alien elements in the Castle District are the metal framed windows and the façade of flowing mortar on one of the corner houses on Tóth Árpád Walkway (38, Úri Street); but despite these new features, this two-storied apartment building harmonizes with the row of historical houses. The use of opening or sliding shutters on the windows of some façades is another feature which harmonizes with the surrounding buildings. In contrast to the attitude of some designers who attempt to distinguish their work, at all cost by stressing individuality, in this case, the simple features mentioned above are much more worthy of praise.

"The past in the future", the utilization of monuments in the city of the future is a fundamental task. The neglected remains must be brought to life, and to do this the old must be filled with new content. This does not mean, however, that every restored monument in Castle District has to be transformed into a museum, although there are plenty of examples of this in Buda. For instance, there is the Museum of Public Catering at 2, Szentháromság Street and 2, Fortuna Street, The Bartók Archives at 9, Országház Street, the Pharmacy Museum at 18, Tárnok Street, the War History Museum at Kapisztrán Square. Above all, there is the former royal palace complex that houses the Budapest Historical Museum, the National Gallery, and the Museum of Modern History, and will also house the National Széchényi Library. Besides these, the National Archives is located in the Castle area, as is the former Erdődy palace on Táncsics Street which, after restoration is completed, will also be used for cultural purposes. Too many museums, however, are inanimating the complex. That is why institutions are located in Castle District, including various branches of the Archives, the different institutes of the Hungarian Academy of Sciences, the National Institution for the Preservation of Historic Monuments, and several planning offices. It is important, though, that enough dwellings remain as well, **36** which, together with the stores, the pharmacy, day-care centres, nursery, schools and restaurants, comprise the framework for daily life in the Buda Castle. The musical and artistic programs are also part of this life, nor is the presence of a hotel necessarily at odds with the new "content" of life in the Castle area.

The new Hilton Hotel is criticised by many for its size, which covers two blocks. In fact, this is its principal drawback. However, the following must be taken into consideration. The author has helped with much of the restoration of the Castle District in Buda, ranging from the detailed plan he prepared in 1948 for the development of the area to working on various aspects of the monuments. For 30 years he has worked to establish the unique character of the Castle area, and the measures that would preserve it. In the historical complex, the measures taken for public lighting, posters, advertisements, benches, street signs, house numbers and pavements were quite different from what is customary in other sections of the capital. Nevertheless, he became an advocate of the Hilton Hotel, insisting that it be built in the Castle area, because he recalled the consternation he felt as a young architect upon seeing a pasha's palace gutted by fire in Constantinople in 1938, exactly 20 years after World War I, and that palace was not even located in an exposed portion of the metropolis. We, however, have been unable for over thirty years to find a suitable investor for this portion of Buda. The Late Baroque façade of the old Ministry of Finance building in Hess András Square, which had survived almost like a theatre prop in front of the burned-out building, had to be preserved because of its historical value. But this was difficult to incorporate into a modern building. What contractor could be required to maintain and display the tower of the medieval Church of St. Nicholas and the northern wall of its nave—containing three Romanesque windows—along with the recently discovered cloister and Renaissance fountain? The former building of the Ministry of Finance (south of the Nicholas Tower), which was rebuilt several times, and the former building of the Szilágyi Erzsébet Gymnasium for Girls (north of the tower), demolished around 1936, were already much larger in mass than the standard scale of the Castle dwellings.

The hotel did not require a greater mass than that of the former Baroque buildings, and it was impossible to subdivide the lots which had been unified in the Baroque period. In this historical environment, it was possible to persuade the builders to disregard their usual architectural plans, that is, a multistory, tower-like building with a swimming pool located on the top, and so on. Instead, they were willing to accept a roof that was in accordance with the regulations for monuments, so that the crest of the building was no higher than the contour lines of the former Ministry of Finance building rising behind it. In this way, the large Baroque façade, the medieval cloister, St. Nicholas's tower, the wall of the church, and the Renaissance fountain could all be reclaimed and even displayed by inclusion in the building programme of the new hotel. These are now elements of a refined building complex, and the lovely atmosphere of the Castle quarter is no longer spoiled by the burnt-out ruins beside the Church of Our Lady.

Frigyes Schulek was the master architect of the *Halászbástya* (Fishermen's Bastion) which was built between 1895 and 1902. This expansive, neo-Romanesque ensemble is a worthy frame for the Church of Our Lady. Schulek dressed the modest brick walls of the fishermen's Bastion of *Víziváros* (Water Town) in a new architectural casing, incorporating the so-called Jesuit Steps, which once had led up to the church. In the small *St. István* (Stephen) Square that was formed there, he placed Alajos Stróbl's equestrian statue of St. Stephen, first king of Hungary—and in the walls of the steps leading to the square, he carved niches for the statues of the leaders of the Hungarian Conquest.

From the upper walkway of the Fishermen's Bastion there is a beautiful view of the capital, which includes the House of Parliament, the Danube with its bridges, and Margaret Island at our feet. From here we can see the uniformly regulated height of the city's buildings.

It is also possible to see the new housing developments built after 1945 which embrace the city's inner nucleus from much further out; the tall blocks shoot up in Óbuda, and can be followed as they circle Pest until they end again on the Buda side with the Kelenföld and Lágymányos housing developments.

Walking among the Castle streets everyone notices the colourful street scenes. This has a historical basis, for the medieval streetscape was strikingly colourful. Not only was the clothing of the nobles, their attendants, and their servants colourful, but so were the interiors and exteriors of the buildings. The medieval façades were decorated by hat-size geometric patterns—squares, hexagons, circles—that were variations of white, black, green, and other colours, and sometimes their paintings simply imitated ashlar or diamond-shaped stones. This can be seen on the façade of 14, Tárnok Street, but such colourful patterns were found elsewhere in the medieval city as well.

38

The Baroque period retained the bright, contrasting colours, but added no new patterns. In most cases the different building components were painted with different colours: for example, the base of Batthyány Palace at 3, Dísz Square was painted with black and yellow stripes.

Classicism used only delicate colours, but four or five pastels were in use earlier. This can be determined from the plans that were submitted to the Pest Committee for Beautification for approval. Romanticism and early eclecticism favoured single coloured façades, especially those of pale-purple, pink and light-green. Only in Late Eclecticism at the turn of the century did the dirty grey colouring of the façades become common. This gave the houses at the beginning the colouring they would eventually have after a few years of pollution.

Thus the colourful effect of the Castle District of Buda can be traced back to historical sources. So can the method of pebble-dashing, which came into use after the city's great fire in 1726 and with which the lower portions of the façades were prepared. There was also a robust ochre colouring which dominated at that time. It was called Habsburg yellow, even though there was no connection to the ruling Habsburg house, but rather, it came into use because of the colour-fast properties of the natural earth colour.

A detailed plan for paving Buda was prepared that was to employ several kinds of cobble stones, asphalt patches bordered by stones, along with the stones that were one time used for covering manholes. Unfortunately, contrary to this plan, bleak concrete and asphalt were laid in Úri Street. Elsewhere, there can be seen small, uniform cobble stones whose crevices were poured too thickly, and as a result the pavement was smeared with asphalt. There is still much to do in the future, including the paving of doorways that do not meet the exacting standards of the buildings.

A pleasant exception to this is the "furnishings" of the Tóth Árpád Walkway, which looks onto Buda Hills. The fresh strip of green laid in the shadow of two rows of trees, the restrained arrangement of bushes and benches, the paving formed of simple but varied materials, and the alternation of planters and flower beds are all excellent ways to furnish a street with uncomplicated good taste which, at the same time, adapts itself to the historical atmosphere.

However, the same cannot be said of the peculiar fountain, a gift from the town of Pécs, that was placed on the walkway. Buda's Castle District is not the most suitable place to deposit works of art, even those of our most famous artists. A fountain sculpture here and there can have a pleasant effect, especially if water flows out of it; a few small statues placed in niches in the courtyards can be lovely too. But we have to be careful not to place an artistic creation on every corner, for such profusion can easily interfere with the effectiveness and full play of the environment. Moderation must be kept in the Castle area.

In conclusion, we urge the reader to come and visit the Castle area often. Walk the Castle streets again and again, during the day and night, in sunlight and moonlight, and even in snow. Take a look into the doorways and around the courtyards, and notice the balanced way of life of those who live here. Sniff the north breeze blowing from the Buda Hills, and take the time to visit the wine cellar of at least one restaurant for a glass of wine. And if sometime the topic should turn to the preservation and evaluation of another historical or simply pleasant section of a town, keep in mind what has been said here, and remember the Castle District of Buda.

List of Plates

1. View of Buda Castle from Gellért Hill
2. Green-glazed stove tile from the age of King Sigismund from the medieval royal palace
3. The enclosed South Courtyard of the Palace
4. The restored gate leading from the South Bastion into the Castle
5. The enclosed South Courtyard viewed from the Gothic Great Hall towards the Mace Tower
6. A head of a Gothic statue from the 1974 findings
7. Statues from the 1974 findings displayed in the Gothic Great Hall
8. Detail of Gothic statue from the 1974 findings
9. The restored sanctuary of the Palace chapel
10. Colourful floor tiles displaying the emblems of King Matthias and the House of Aragon (about 1450)
11. A fragment of a Renaissance ledge from King Matthias' palace
12. The Renaissance fountain in the South Garden with Matthias' and Beatrice's coat of arms
13. The King's Basement with the restored Gothic balcony
14. Gothic *sedilia*, 4–5, Dísz (Parade) Square
15. A row of Baroque houses, 12–15, Dísz (Parade) Square
16. A patterned façade with painted medieval decoration, 14, Tárnok Street
17. Houses with restored Gothic façades, 14–16, Tárnok Street
18. Short, narrow alleyways like Hajadon Street link the larger, longer streets
19. Úri Street, the longest street in the dwelling quarter of Buda
20. Gothic *sedilia*, 13, Tárnok Street
21. Balta köz (Balta Alleyway)
22. A Gothic house with three surviving stories, 31, Úri Street
23. Gothic arcades from the 15th century, 2, Országház Street
24. Gothic details on the house at 20, Országház Street
25. Gothic houses from the turn of the 14th–15th centuries, 18–22, Országház Street
26. The 14th-century tombstone of the painter Abel
27. The Church of Our Lady (Matthias Church) and surroundings around 1880

55. The former House of Parliament which presently houses various institutions of the Hungarian Academy of Sciences, 28, Országház Street
56. Gothic synagogue, 18, Táncsics Street
57. Baroque pharmacy, 18, Tárnok Street
58. Details of a Baroque portal, 1, Táncsics Street
59. Táncsics Street with the headquarters of the National Institute for the Preservation of Historic Monuments in the foreground
60. The interior of the National Institute for the Preservation of Monuments, 1, Táncsics Street
61. Old castle walls and the new houses on Castle Hill facing the Danube
62. The Danube façade of the Hilton Hotel with the remains of the Church of St. Nicholas
63. Detail of the Danube façade of the Hilton Hotel
64. A new apartment house, 15, Tárnok Street
65. The Gothic vaults of the Alabárdos Restaurant, 2, Országház Street
66. The wine cellar of the Régi Országház (Old Parliament) Restaurant, 17, Országház Street
67. The highest tower of the Halászbástya (Fishermen's Bastion)
68. The statue of St. Stephen in the Halászbástya (Fishermen's Bastion)
69. The castle wall and a row of houses on the western side of Castle Hill
70. Tóth Árpád Walkway just inside the western portion of the castle wall
71. The Church of Our Lady (Matthias Church) and the Buda Castle as seen from the tower of St. Nicholas's Church
72. The coat of arms of the town of Buda

Plates

10, 11

18, 19

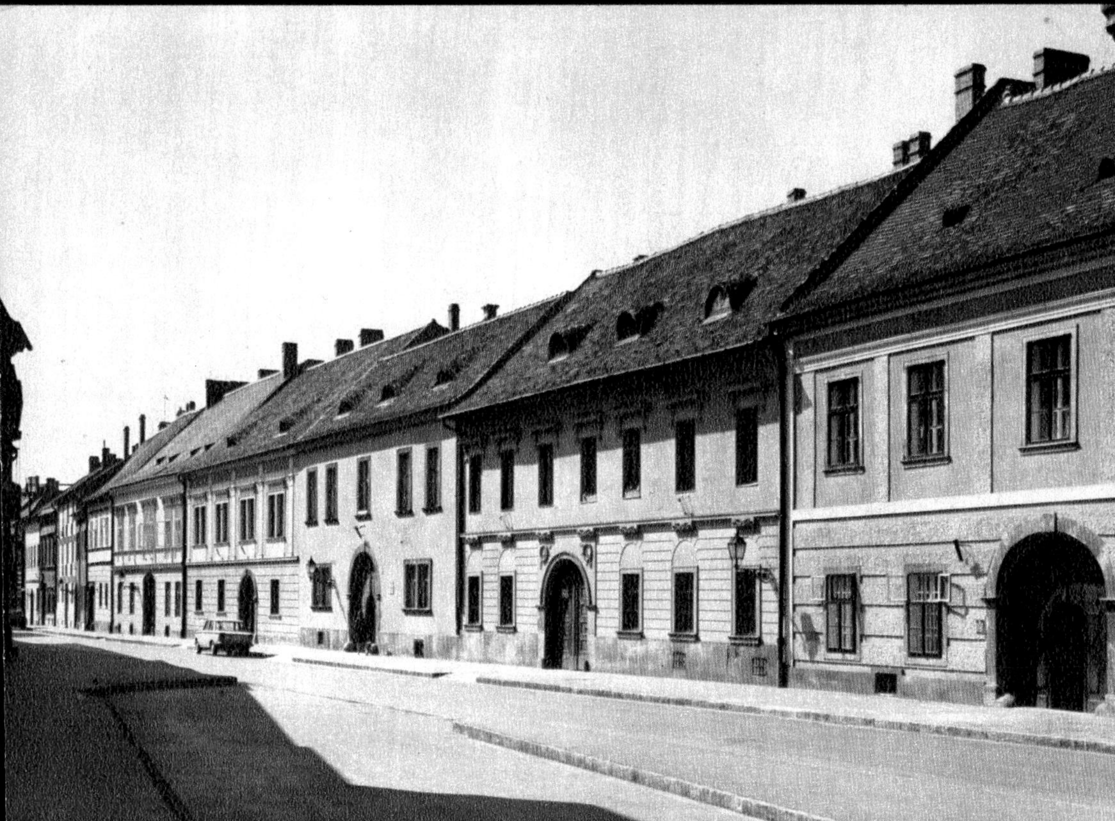

20, 21

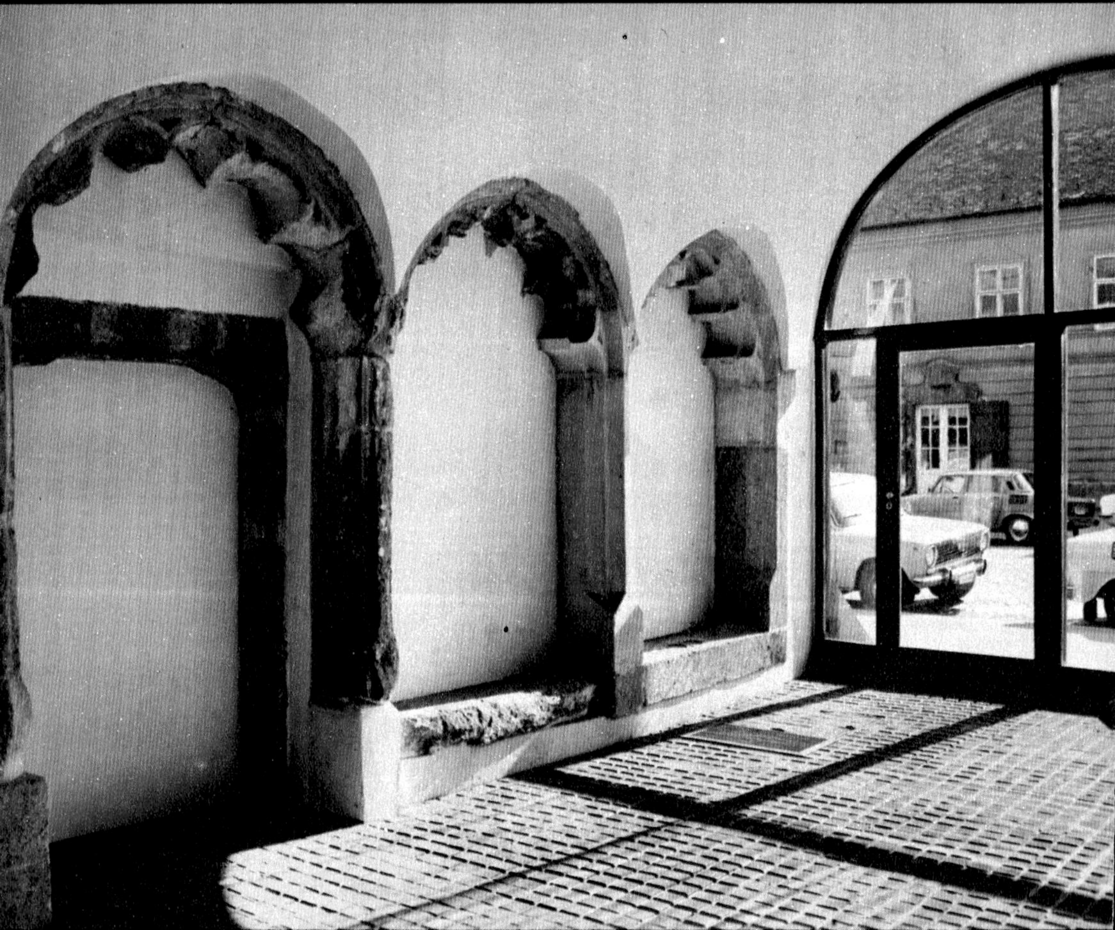

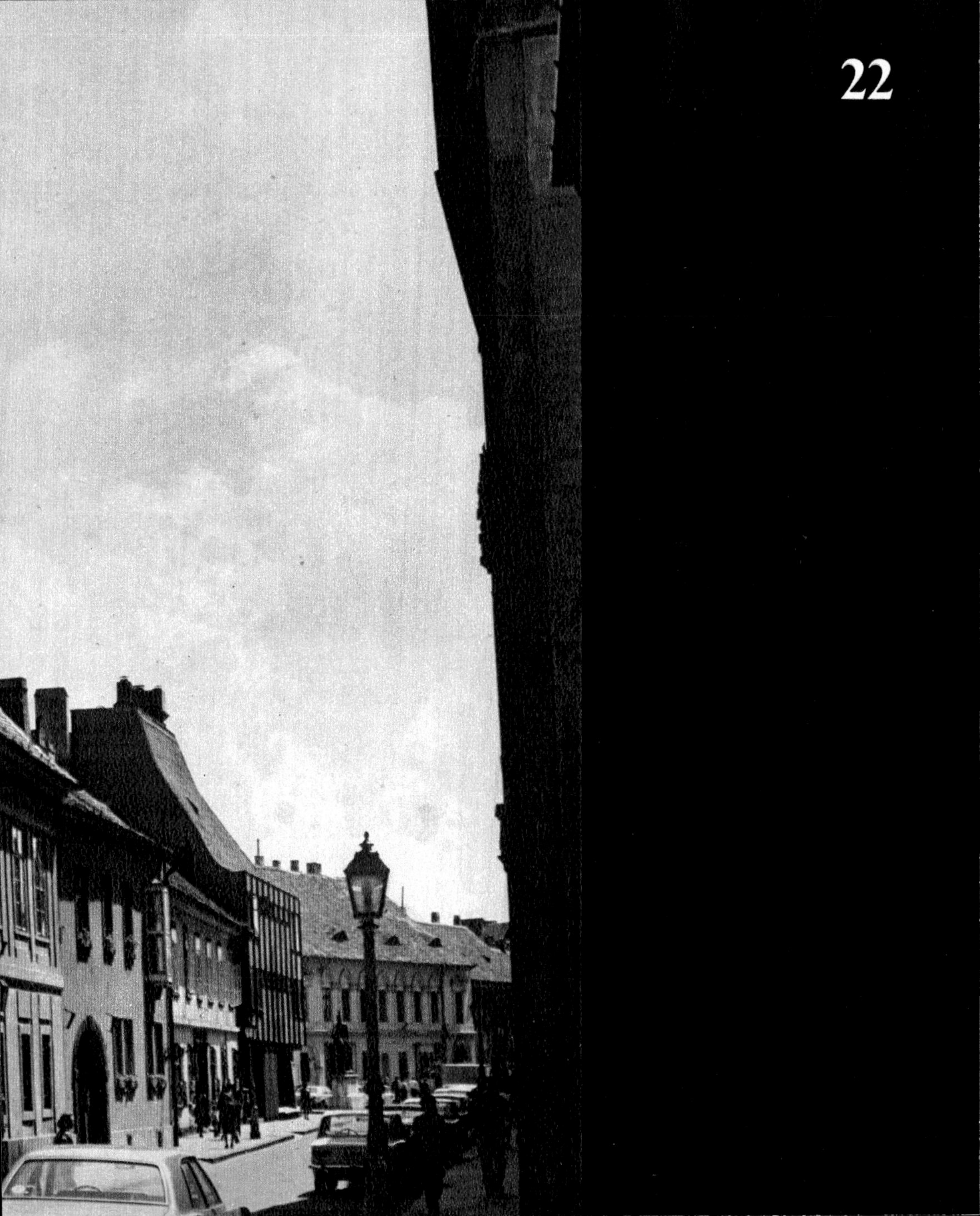

22

28

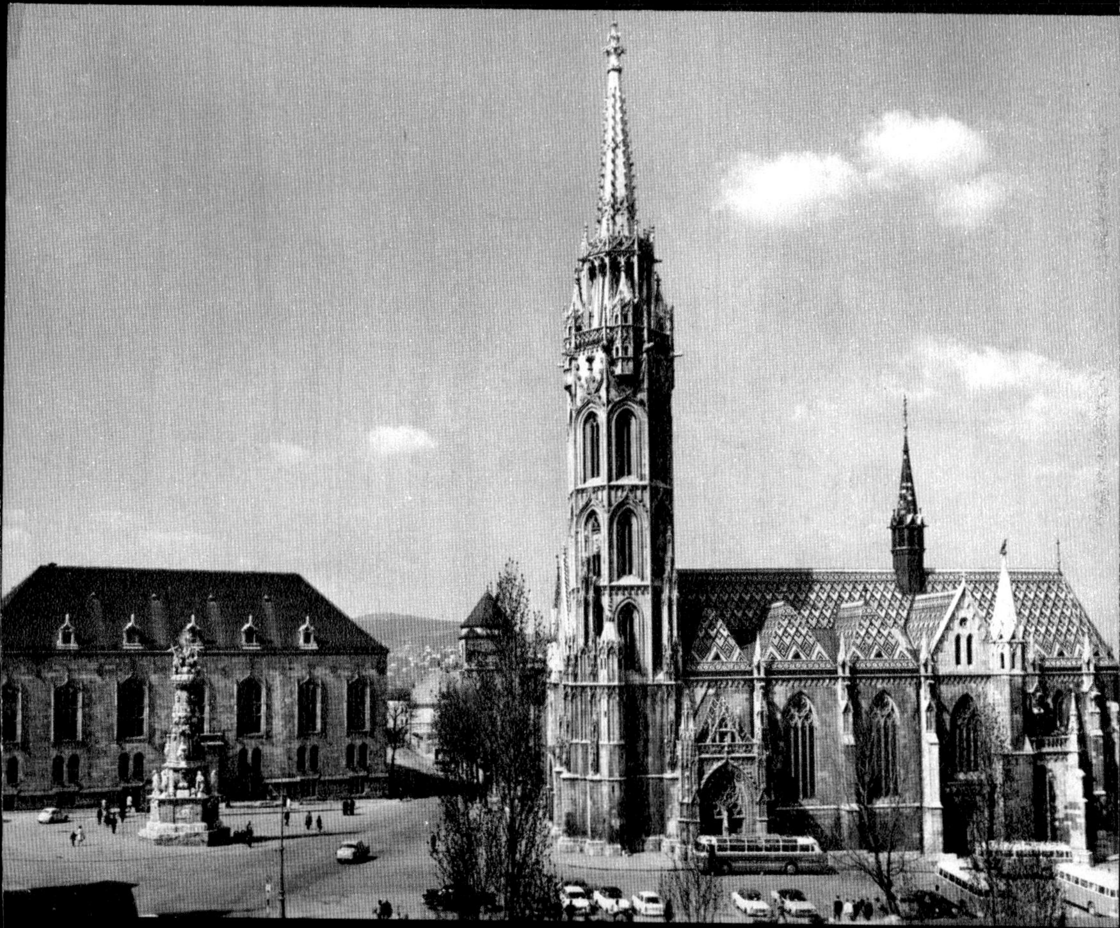

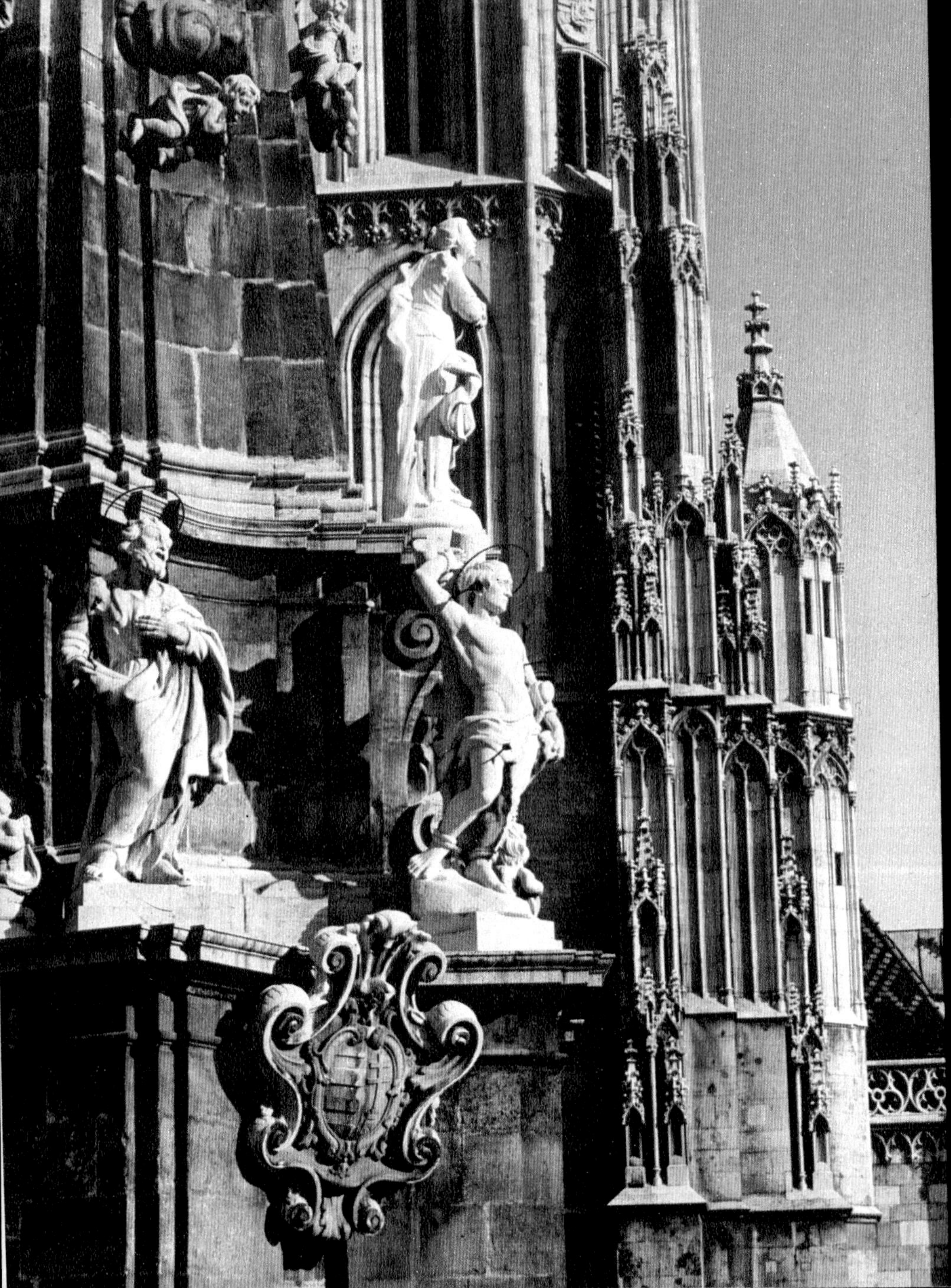

31
32

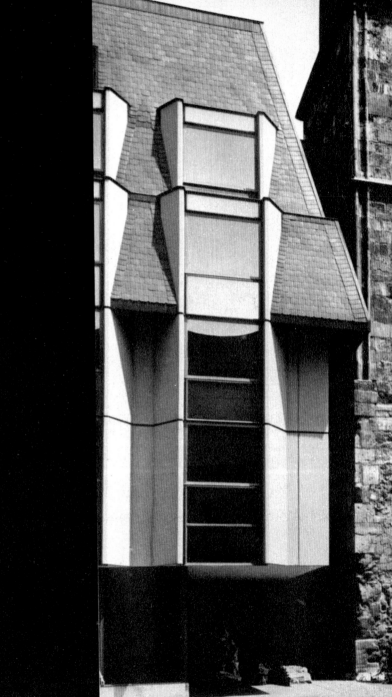

39

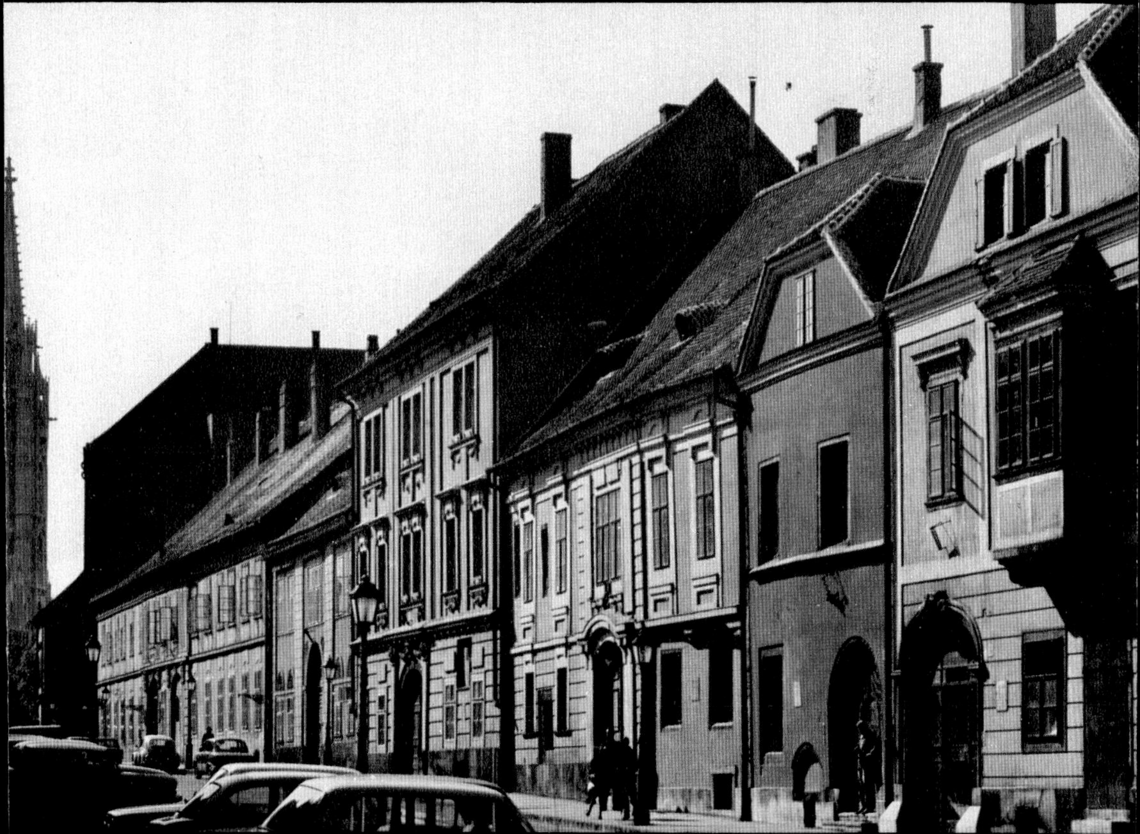

56
57

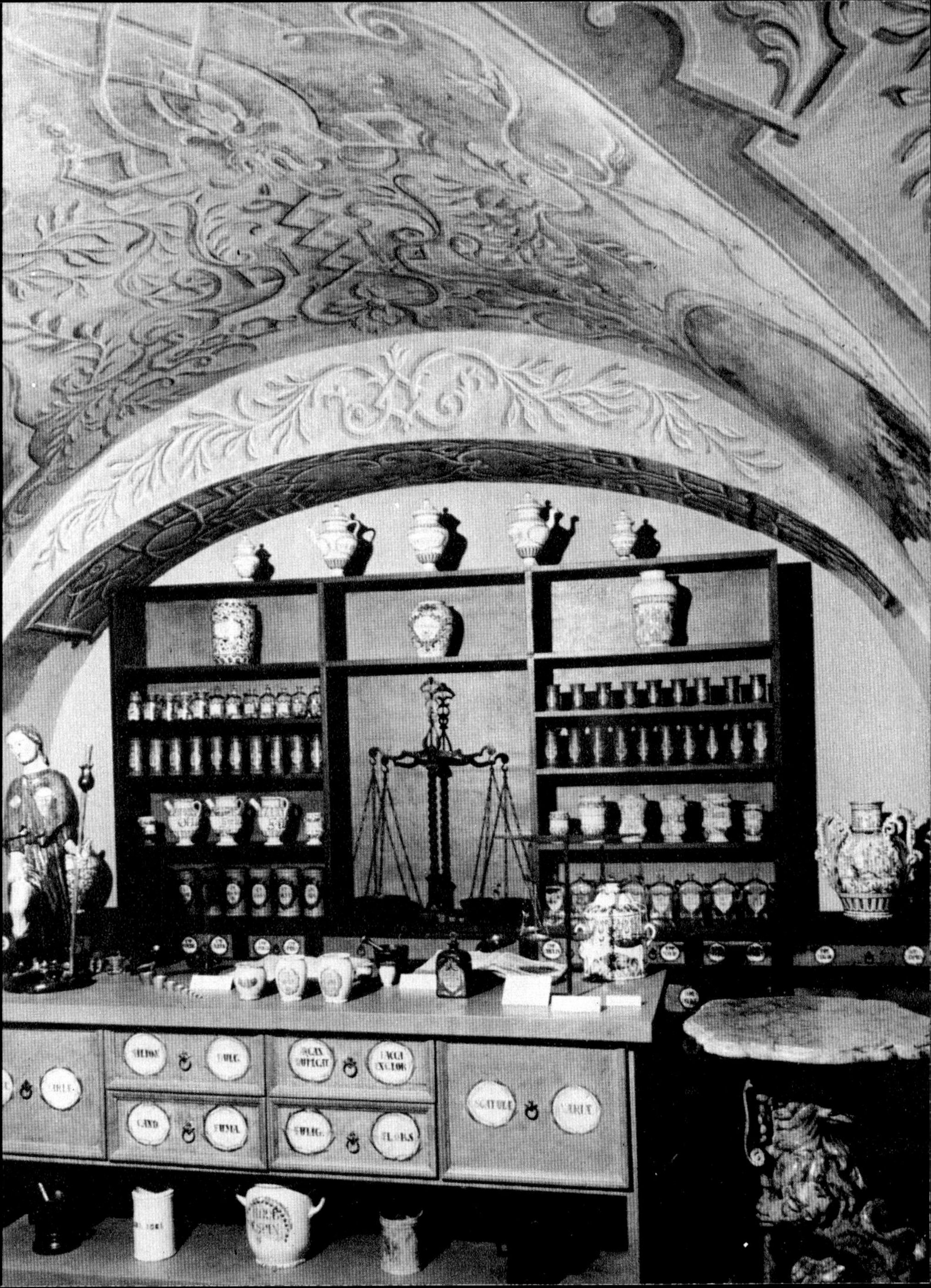

65
66

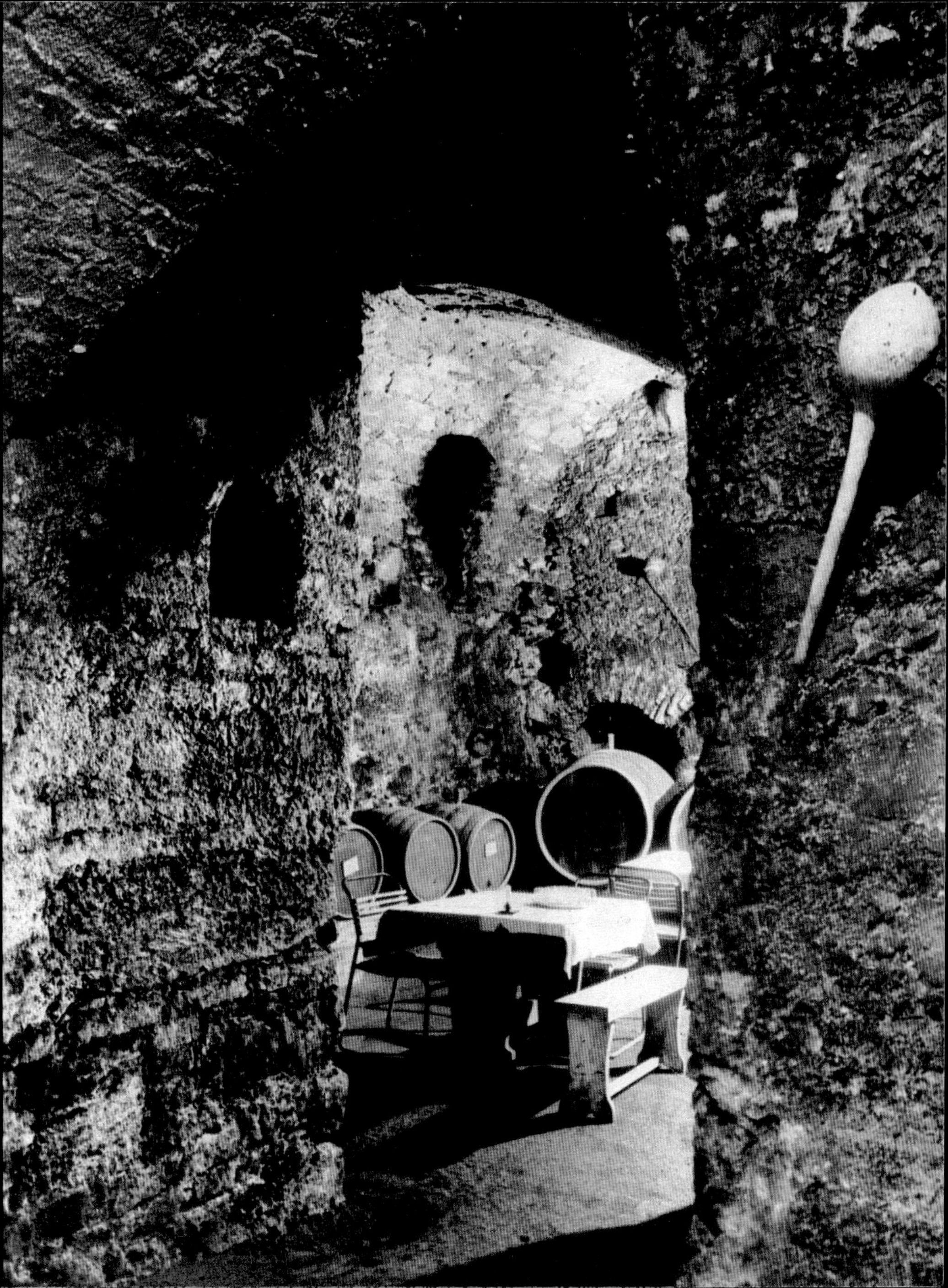

69

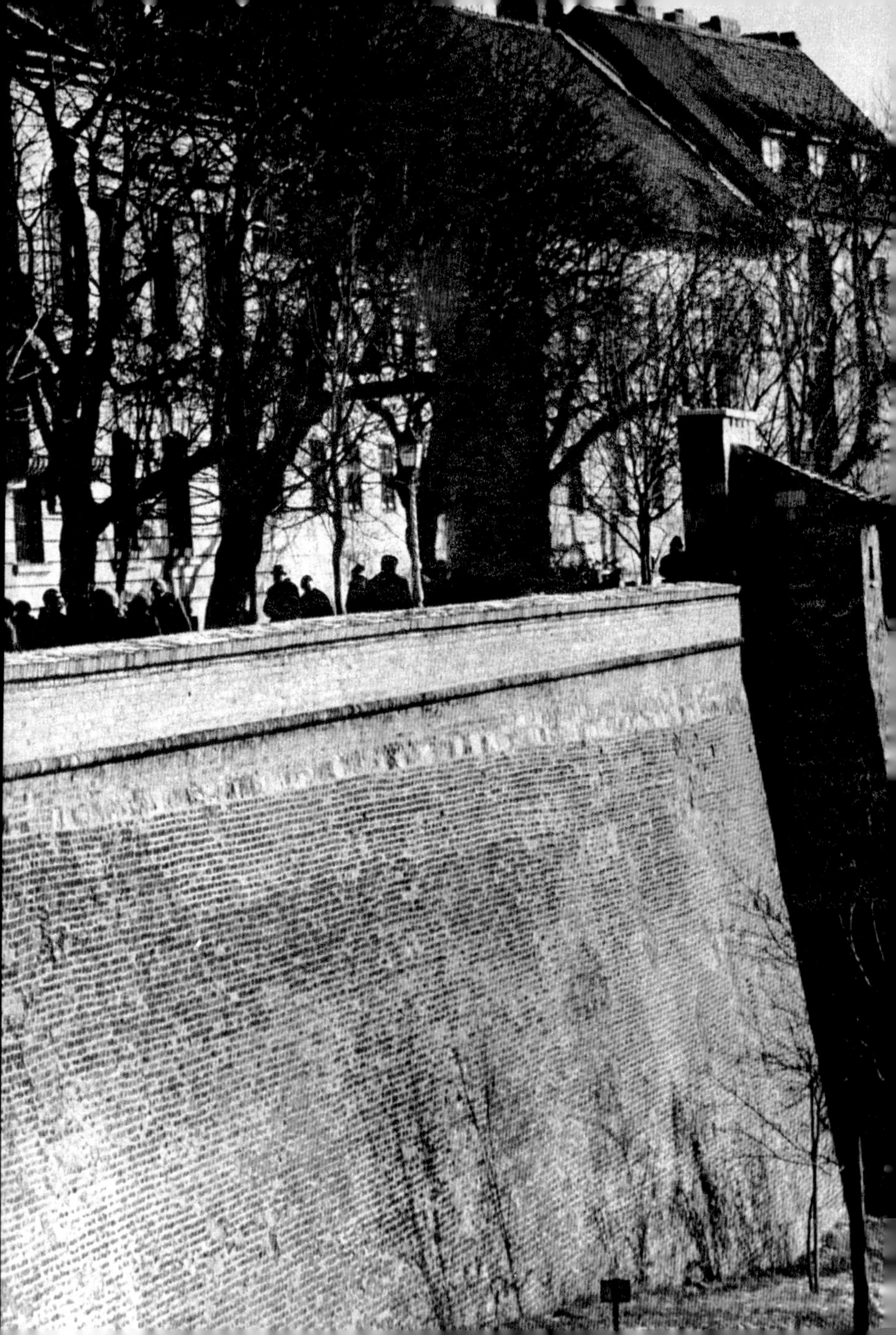